5 THINGS WOMEN NEED TO KNOW ABOUT THE MEN THEY DATE

Steven Kerry Brown, Private Investigator

PREFACE

This book is not a work of fiction. It is based on true cases worked by the author. The names, locations, amounts of money involved, and in some instances other details have been changed to protect the privacy of my clients and also those scumbags who took advantage of my clients.

No part of this book may be reproduced or transmitted in any form or by any electronic or mechanical means, including photocopying, recording, or by any information storage and retrieval system without the express written permission and consent of the author.

ACKNOWLEDGMENTS

I'd like to thank my son Steven Kerry Brown II for all of his input and help with the website for this book. Kudos to Stephanie Farnsworth for copy edit, Barrett Biggers for the cover design, and as always to my wife Melanie for her patience in putting up with the millions of questions I ask her as to which sentence sounds better or which cover design is best. Also to Brookie Brown, Kjristi Brown, Leah Garriott, Vinnie and Melissa Dunne, Kacey Pernell, Cheryl Stelk, Benjamin Brown, and about 150 others that had input into the cover design of this book.

Also I need to acknowledge my clients, who shall remain anonymous, even though they have given permission for me to use their stories as examples of what not to do.

And as usual I give a special thanks to James Frey who taught me about writing. I especially wish to acknowledge the assistance of Frank Green who also copy edited and helped format this book, as well as being my mentor in the craft of writing.

TABLE OF CONTENTS

CHAPTER ONE

FIVE QUESTIONS TO ASK

HOW CAN YOU FIND THE ANSWERS YOU NEED?

Laurel called me. She'd known Ross for over a year but they'd been dating for only four months. The relationship had deepened but Laurel had some lingering doubts about him. Some things he did and said didn't jibe with what she knew about him.

She had just turned fifty and had three teenage girls at home. Her deadbeat ex-husband recently married a woman fifteen years his junior. Now she had Ross who said he was fifty-four years old. He told her he'd married for the first time when he was forty-nine, but was now divorced. Did he really have an earlier marriage? she wondered. Was he really divorced? She'd seen him fill out a medical insurance form one night and in the space for marital status he'd written "other." What the heck did that mean? Separated maybe? Did he have kids from an earlier marriage? He never spoke about them if he did.

So Laurel called me wanting answers to her questions.

"Why don't you ask him?" I said.

"Because he already told me he was divorced, and I don't want him to think I don't trust him."

"But you don't trust him," I said. Whatever happened to honesty in a relationship? I thought. But I didn't say that.

"Yes," she said. "But he doesn't know I'm calling you."

"Which is why," I said, "we're called private investigators and not something like public broadcasters."

I told her she could find the answers to her questions for herself if she wished, and I'd tell her how. But she didn't have the time so I took a $250 retainer on her credit card and started the search.

IS HE MARRIED?

The one question, "Is his divorce final?" pops up more often than any other question in premarital investigations.

- Has the man you've been corresponding with or dating, maybe misled you a little?
- Has he given some indication that he hasn't been telling you the entire truth?
- You want children and he says, "Been there, done that." But he never mentions the kids' mother. What does that tell you?

Why was it so hard for Laurel to simply ask him the questions she wanted him to answer? Well, I suppose she didn't want to seem more interested in him than he was in her. Yet, she knew she was already falling for this guy.

The way Laurel's story ended up was very interesting. We'll get to her story in chapter three.

IS HE FINANCIALLY STABLE?

What else do women need to know? It's important to know if your potential mate is financially stable. You don't want to become heavily involved with someone who is going to suck your bank account dry. I'm not suggesting you are a gold digger, but you need to know the facts.

In the old days, you could ask a friend at a real estate property management office to pull a credit report on the guy you're seeing. Not today. You can, but your friend will probably lose their job when your boyfriend calls up ABC Realtor and asks why they pulled his credit. People are with good reason much more aware these days about inquiries into their credit history. Too many inquiries into a person's credit worthiness, causes a credit score to nosedive.

If someone has several inquires to the credit bureau, he must need the money and is not as credit-worthy as someone who doesn't need the money. Makes a lot sense, doesn't it? Just like the old saw: A bank will give you a loan if you don't need it but if you do, they won't. Go figure.

But how do you find out if your potential mate is a man of means or if he lives in the basement of his mother's house? We'll explore ways to answer that in chapter six.

DOES HE HAVE A CRIMINAL RECORD?

Why do you care if the person you're dating has a criminal record? Hasn't everybody had a few scrapes with the law? No, not really.

I worked on a case a while back where one of the things we wanted to get was the 911call log from a particular residence. This was a child custody issue, and the new stepmother and the seventeen-year-old stepson weren't hitting it off too well. The teenager was really mad at this woman for replacing his mother. This woman had been having an affair with the boy's father while he was still married to his mother, and as soon as the divorce was final he married the new woman. No wonder the boy was so mad at her. The stepmother and the boy had a few arguments and she'd called the police more than once.

I pulled the logs of the 911 calls from the residence where the stepmother and the seventeen-year-old now lived. Eleven calls in three months. How many times have you called 911? Not that many, I expect. Police logs and 911 calls are a good indication of something amiss.

You need to know if the man of your dreams is the stuff of nightmares. Is he your prince or a felon? Does he have a violent past? Does he have any arrests or domestic violence injunctions? Do you want to live with someone that is going to beat you?

Has he had arrests for bad checks? A series of worthless check charges might be an indicator of dishonesty, unreliability, and financial instability. A worthless check over $150 is a felony in the state of Florida. You should find out if the man you're thinking of moving in with has just recently vacated an abode with bars over the windows and electronic locks. You'll find out all about this in chapter four.

DOES HE DRINK ALCOHOL TO EXCESS?

Everyone drinks, right? Well, maybe, maybe not. But does everyone drink to excess?

Have you ever lived with an alcoholic? I wish I could impress on people that have no personal knowledge of alcoholism just how much fun it is to live with an alcoholic. They lie, they steal, they leave half-filled glasses of vodka hidden under the bathroom sink so when you throw out all of the booze in the house, they still have their stashes. Did I also mention they lie?

"Oh, I've had nothing to drink today, honey. I promise."

You can smell it oozing out of their pores, and they can't walk a straight line. Oh yeah, living with an alcoholic is just loads of fun. And do you want someone who drinks excessively driving your kids to school?

So how do you find out if Mr. Right is really Mr. Wrong when it comes to alcohol abuse? As you'll see, there are several ways to get the answer to that question. I'll show you how in chapter seven.

DOES HE USE DRUGS?

Does your new partner use drugs? I've seen more relationships destroyed from drug abuse than any other single misdeed. If the person you're considering sharing your future with uses illegal drugs or even prescription drugs, don't continue to carry on with him. Walk away. Find out before you've invested a lot of time in this relationship.

Recreational use of illegal drugs often escalates into drug dependency. I've seen lives and families ruined. In one case the parents began sniffing glue as teenagers. Things escalated to prescription drugs and then to cocaine. Today, both parents are in jail and two out of their three children are divorced and in jail. Those two children are in the state penitentiary for terms of eight and fifteen years for distributing minor amounts of prescription drugs to feed their own habits—habits they learned from their parents.

Learn from Amy's story: She was a fun-loving single female who is a professional in the healthcare field. She began dating a fellow who introduced her to cocaine. Four months later she began calling in too sick to work. When she did go to work she showed up disheveled and late. Dating this fellow nearly cost her that $200,000-a-year job. Plus he stole $21,000 from her. Even worse, during their "courtship," she'd spent nearly $25,000 on the drugs. Amy had no drug habit or even any drug use prior to meeting "the love of her life."

You probably think there is no way short of drug testing or having a heart-to-heart with your new lover's sibling to find out early on in a relationship if the guy you might seriously consider as a mate has a drug problem. Wrong! There are several ways to get the answer to that question. I'll show you how in chapter seven.

Let's recap the five things you need to know about the guy you're dating.

THE SHORT LIST

♦ **Is his divorce final?** Or is he still legally married?
♦ **Is he financially stable?** Does he know how to manage money? You don't want some guy that is going to drain your bank account.

♦ **Does he have a criminal record?** If you have children from a previous marriage just having another man in the house will usually create problems; but if he's a convicted felon, you've really got trouble. And if he has domestic violence convictions or restraining orders against him, your safety is at stake.

♦ **Does he drink alcohol to excess?** What's excess? If you're asking yourself this question then the answer is probably yes.

♦ **Is he involved in the drug trade?** Does he use illegal drugs such as cocaine, marijuana, meth? Is he addicted to prescription narcotics like oxycotin or hydrocodone?

CHAPTER 2

IS THE DIVORCE FINAL?

I worked a case for Susan several years ago. She was dating Ted. He resided in another city but traveled to north Florida so frequently that he bought a condo and furnished it. Mary Beth and he became inseparable during non-working hours. He would give her gifts and even bought her a new Mercedes.

When he had trade shows to attend in Las Vegas or other resort destinations, and she could wrangle the time off, she'd travel with him. She became very emotionally attached to him. She was thirty-two, never married, and thoughts of family and children flitted through her mind.

As she began to push about visiting him in south Florida, where he had a permanent residence, he would waffle. "Not next weekend, Susan. I have appointments."

She began to wonder if he really was single. So she called me.

It took me only about forty minutes to get his wife's name, Rose, the address of their marital home in south Florida, and the phone number there.

I think she already knew the answer to her questions. She could have found all of that information herself fairly easily and saved my fee. I'll show you how you can, too.

As for Susan, she went right over to his condo in north Florida and knocked on the door. She dialed the wife's phone on her cell and when he came to the door she pushed "Send." His wife, of course, heard all of the conversation between her and Ted. After a minute she handed the phone to Ted.

"Who's that?" Ted said.

"Rose," Susan said, and watched as his face turned ashen.

He mumbled something about calling her back in a minute and tossed the phone at Susan as she left. She drove away in the Mercedes waving at him while he stood in the front door. A few days later he called her and said he wanted her to return the Mercedes. She refused, and they went to court. Even though Ted still owed a substantial amount of money on the car, the judge ruled the car was a gift and, as such, Susan was entitled to keep the vehicle.

LIGHTNING DOES STRIKE TWICE

Fast-forward a couple of years: Susan is now thirty-five. Ted has paid off the Mercedes, and she holds the title to it. She has been dating Ralph and is madly in love with him. They're engaged and the wedding is in two weeks. Ralph, an accountant from Los Angeles, also owns some property in La Jolla. She believes Ralph to be forty. He's so attractive and so nice she wonders why he never married before. "I just never found the right woman," he says. "Until now, that is."

One night, while Ralph was in the shower she picked up his billfold and thumbed through it. Inside she found a photo of three children between the ages of ten and fifteen. She slipped it back into the wallet and said nothing to him. But after he left for work she called me.

"Steve," she said, "Remember me? Susan? Well, I'm getting married in two weeks, and I'm afraid that my fiancé may have children he's never told me about."

"How about a wife he's never told you about?" I said to her.

"Well, maybe that too," she said.

FINDING THE MARRIAGE OR DIVORCE

So, how can you find out if the guy you're dating is single or married? Obtaining marriage and divorce records is probably one of the most difficult tasks we'll tackle in this book. There are three main routes to this information.

♦ Civil records in the county courthouse where the divorce occurred.

♦ Certificates of Marriages in the county courthouse where you think the ceremony might have taken place.

♦ Property records where the guy lives or lived previously.

DIVORCE

In most states, divorce records are public, but there are some states like New York where the divorce files are confidential. Even if the divorce file is not public, the fact that a person received what is called a Judgment of Divorce or a Final Judgment of Divorce is almost always public. But you have to know how and where to look. At our website you can request that we conduct a civil search for you.

Go to www.5ThingsWomenNeedToKnow.com. Or you can follow the instructions below for free.

The most direct route to finding out if there really was a divorce is to search the records in the county where the divorce is alleged to have transpired. One way to find that divorce record, if it exists, is to Google "Clerk of the Court" and add the name of the county where you want to search. If you don't know the name of the county, but know the name of the city, then another Google search will give you the city-county combination. Don't forget we have Orange County, California and Orange County, Florida, so make sure you have the right county-state combination.

You'll see a list of references to that particular city and county. Search for the clerk of the court of that county. Not all states have counties. Louisiana has parishes. Not all counties are on line but many are.

If you don't have any luck using your favorite Internet search engine, try this tip: Become familiar with BRB (Business Resources Bureau) and their publications. They maintain a free side to their website at http://www.brbpublications.com

Once on the site, find "Use These Free Resources." Click on "Links to Thousands of Free Public Record Sites." No, it's not a come-on in an attempt to up-sell you like most other "free data search" sites. There are only two privately run websites that I recommend. This is one of them. The other is at www.5ThingsWomenNeedToKnow.com

Now back to BRB: Once you've clicked on "Use These Free Resources," you'll see "State, County, and City Sites." Click on the state you're interested in and try to locate the Family Law Civil section where divorce files are usually listed. If you can't find the Family Law section, check for the *recorder's office* or *official records*. There you may find the final judgment of divorce.

Many states are enforcing additional privacy issues and may require you to view the record in person instead of viewing it online. The pendulum has been swinging away from making all records publically available online. But, generally the records are still public. So if you find a judgment of divorce but can't see it and the record you want is in Los Angeles and you're in New York, what are you to do?

Click on http://www.brbpublications.com/prrn/default.aspx

BRB maintains a list called, "Public Record Retriever Network" (PRRN). You can find a public record retriever in almost any county that will, for a small fee, go to the county courthouse, pull the record you want, and fax or email a copy to you. Or call us at 904-819-9700 and we'll get it for you.

But search the list for yourself first and see if you can find it for free.

Okay, so you've searched and can't find the county divorce records on line. Then pick up the phone and call the Clerk of the Court and ask if final judgments of divorce, or if "divorce actions" are available online. If the answer is no, don't hang up. You'll be surprised how helpful some clerks at the courthouses are. Ask the person you're talking to if they would do you a big favor. Tell them the truth. Tell them you're dating a guy who says he was divorced in their county but you have your doubts and want to make sure. "Would you please do me a huge favor and check your index to see if there was a divorce?" The clerk will tell you they don't do record checks over the phone, but nine times out of ten the clerk will make an exception in your case. It's usually just that easy.

I don't know of any states that cross-reference marriage licenses between counties; that is, you can't go to one county and see all the marriage licenses throughout the state. In some states you can go to State Bureau of Vital Records and you'll find a complete list of marriages within their state. In some states like Florida, you can even search their records by the wife's maiden name. Florida is a "public record state" but many states aren't. That means by law, all state or government records are considered open for public viewing. Here is Title X, Chapter 119.01 of Florida Statutes:

General state policy on public records.—

(1) It is the policy of this state that all state, county, and municipal records are open for personal inspection and copying by any person. Providing access to public records is a duty of each agency.

I wish all states had similar statutes. Of course, as you probably won't be surprised to know, even in Florida there are many exceptions to such a statute. Still, most state, county, and city records are available to be examined and copied.

DID SUSAN GET MARRIED?

So what happened to Susan?

Well, I went to work with the information she gave me. In a few hours I found out that Ralph indeed had three children and a wife who thought she was still married to him. He'd previously had a good business going in southern California. One weekend he sent his wife and kids down to La Jolla to list the condo there for sale. When the family returned to Los Angeles, Ralph was gone. The wife filed a missing person report and had heard nothing about him or from him for over a year. She thought maybe he drove off someplace and died but, no, he was in Florida preparing to wed Susan. Can she pick her men or what?

I relayed this information to her, and she said, "Well, I guess we'll have to postpone the wedding."

"Postpone?" I said. "How about cancel?"

"I love him too much to let him go," she said. "He's the love of my life. I've never met anyone like him. We'll just have to get him divorced and then reschedule the wedding."

As far as I know, they're still married, and he hasn't disappeared on her—at least not yet.

THE SHORT LIST

♦ **Check out his divorce file.** If you suspect that your new boyfriend may still have a wife or two hanging around, about 90% of the time such suspicions prove to be accurate.

♦ **Divorce files in most states (but not all) are public records.** In the file you can often find the allegations that led to the divorce as well as the settlements made, amounts of alimony, and child support payments.

♦ **Final Judgments of Divorce are usually located in the official records at your Clerk of the Court where the divorce action was filed.** This can usually be found online without leaving your house. I recommend that you go to the courthouse and have the clerk pull the file so you can see it and get a hard copy. Call before going to the courthouse to review a file and make sure that the file has not been sent to archives. If it has, have them order it so that it'll be there when you go to review it.

♦ **Look through the new boyfriend's billfold or personal correspondence.** If you have suspicions, don't hesitate to follow them up. It may seem sneaky but it may save you from the terrible consequences of being a bigamist's second or even third wife.

♦ **Check property records.** See if he still owns property in both his and his wife's name. Again, the clerk of the court, official records, will show you any deeds and mortgages in his or his wife's name. This is another search you can do in your pajamas.

CHAPTER 3

FINDING THE DIVORCE

Remember Ted, who gave Susan the Mercedes?

How did I find Ted, the lowlife-cheating husband of Rose? Susan told me he lived in Ft. Lauderdale, Florida, which is in Broward County. I went to the Broward County's property appraiser website (it's listed on the BRB Publications Free Resource link), and I searched Ted's name. I was curious as to how much his house was worth as he had enough money to give her a Mercedes. And guess what? The property was held in both Ted and Rose's name.

I searched the clerk of the court official records (see the next section on official records to understand what these are in Broward County) and found the deed in both of their names and no quit claim deed from one to the other which you might expect to find if a divorce had taken place. Plus, I found no divorce for them. Hence, it appeared to me that they were still married.

Quit Claim

Often mispronounced as "quick claim" by people unfamiliar with real estate terms is a document signed by a person stating that they relinquish any interest they may have had to a parcel of land, a home, or any real property. It is often used in divorces where one spouse will relinquish any claim to what was the marital home.

Just to make sure, before I told Susan that the property was in both names, I searched phone listings and found their phone number. I knew Ted was not home because he was in North Florida with Susan, so I called the number and Rose answered. I not only used a pretext as to why I was calling but I also spoofed my phone number, (see paragraph below) and she admitted that she was "Mrs. Ted" and that Ted would be back in town later in the week. It took me maybe thirty minutes of computer time and one long distance phone call to figure it all out. Susan kept the Mercedes. And Ted kept Rose. But I bet Rose was hell for a while.

Pretext

A pretext is basically a plausible lie. It is used in conversations and designed to get the other person to reveal some information about themselves or their mates that normally they would not reveal to strangers.

SPOOFING TELEPHONE NUMBERS

Having the ability to change how your phone number appears on someone else's caller ID screen is a good tool for private investigators. It might come in handy for you if you're doing the investigative work yourself. Basically you subscribe to a spoofing service. There are several of them. I use www.spoofcard.com. You have to buy credits, but they're cheap. For ten bucks you get 60 minutes. The more time you buy at once, the cheaper it is per minute.

You dial the spoof card's number and you're transferred to a computer. It asks you for your PIN number, which you get when you buy the credits. Then it asks for the number you want to call and then the number you want to appear on caller ID. There are other options as well. You can change your voice from a male to a female and vice versa. You can add background noise if you wish. It will also record the call if you want it to.

I don't recommend recording the call because that's illegal in several states. You remember the Monica Lewinsky-Bill Clinton affair and Linda Tripp recording her phone conversations with Monica? Well, in Washington, D.C. where Monica lived there was no rule about recording phone calls. But in Maryland where Linda Tripp resided, there is. Maryland is what we call a two-party or all-party state wherein all parties to a phone conversation have to give permission before anyone records the call. Linda Tripp was prosecuted by Maryland for recording those calls. So, don't record unless you know the state law.

SEARCHING PUBLIC RECORDS

Keep a couple of things in mind when searching public records. Once you get to the Clerk of the Court online, then you want to search civil cases, if you're looking for the divorce. We'll talk about criminal case searches in chapter four.

Usually divorces will be in the higher court. Different states have different court systems, but they are often broken down into higher courts and lower courts. Some have multiple layers of lower courts, so you'll have to do a little researching. If you have the option to choose what kind of case you're looking for at the clerk's website, then you might look for "family law" or "domestic relation" cases. Often, you'll see these abbreviated as FL or FM or DR in the case file number.

Now, sometimes we get in the mode of thinking that websites are perfect, infallible. They're not. For instance, if you search for my name in the county where I was first divorced, the clerk's website returns "no records" of any divorce action. But if you search for that divorce by using my ex-wife's name, you'll see it come up. I don't have an explanation for that. It's just the way it is. So the rule is to double check when you can. If you find what you're looking for then you don't need to go any further. But if you don't find it, search a little more.

As in my case, for whatever reason, my divorce file doesn't show on the clerk's website under the family law section. So if you don't find what you're looking for in the civil file sections then go to the "official records" section and look there.

OFFICIAL RECORDS

What are "official records?" Well, they may not call it "official records" in your county. They call it the "County Recorder's Office" if you're in Arizona. This is the place where deeds and judgments are filed or recorded. Usually liens, judgments, deeds, mortgages, and anything that might affect "real property" are recorded there. Almost always they will have a book and page number. In the old days these deeds and judgments were hand written in a large ledger book and numbered. Hence the book and page number is still in use today.

So in the county where I was divorced, you can search the civil records where you won't find my divorce because of some glitch in the system, or you can go to the official record site where you'll not only find my final judgment of divorce but you can also read and print a copy of the nine page divorce settlement document and see how much I paid in child support and other payments.

So suppose you're dating someone named "Steven Brown," and he told you he was divorced in the county of Contra Costa, California. Well, go to the BRB website and find Contra Costa, California. Click on the Superior Court listing. Not the index, but the court itself. You'll have the option to search for records. Input "Steven Brown" and indicate you don't know when it occurred. You will find a list of Steven Browns and the very first one indicates it is a Dissolution With Children. That Steven Brown is not me, it's just an example but that record is really there. Check it out. In fact on the first page there are four dissolutions by various Steven Browns.

None of which, by the way are me, as I was not divorced in California. If you're searching through all of the Steven Browns, it would be helpful to know the previous wife's name. Hopefully the name you're searching is less common than mine. It's really that simple.

Now, remember Laurel we mentioned in Chapter One? She'd been dating Ross for four months and she was thinking marriage. Ross, who claimed to be fifty-four years old (turned out he was fifty-six—people lie about the strangest things), told her his first marriage was when he was forty-nine and now he was divorced. A short marriage for sure but it just didn't work out. Of course, her question: "Was he really divorced?"

Laurel, being no dummy got Ross drunk one night and got him to tell her the name of his former wife. That's when she called me and I went to work. The name she had given me, "Cheryl Woodruff," was not that common. Plus she knew that this Cheryl had lived in Tampa, Florida, at one time. I used some databases that are available only to private investigators and quickly found her. But I could have done a basic Internet search and found her. The advantage I had was my search also gave me her date of birth, social security number, and other identifiers, so I could distinguish her from any other Cheryl Woodruffs I might come across.

Interestingly, she was using the last name Woodruff and not Ross's last name of Murphy. I searched civil records in Hillsborough County (where Tampa is located) and found Cheryl's divorce from her previous husband Woodruff whose name she was still carrying. Odd, I thought. She probably had children by Woodruff. I later found out she did and carried that name for the sake of the children.

So now I began to look for the divorce between Cheryl and Ross Murphy. I searched everywhere in the state of Florida that I could think to look and couldn't find it. So I thought, okay, I can't find the divorce, so they're probably not divorced. So far I had not done anything that Laurel or you couldn't have done. I used only public record searches. So I decided to look for the marriage. I searched every conceivable place in Florida.

Marriage license applications are almost always public record. Some counties have them online and some do not. But you'll find them available at the courthouses if they're not online.

I called Laurel and told her that not only could I not find the divorce, but I couldn't find her sweetheart's prior marriage either. Of course, if they were married in Las Vegas or the Bahamas or someplace else, then we wouldn't find it without searching those particular places.

Laurel paid my bill and thanked me. Then in a few days she called me back. Ross admitted to her that he had married Cheryl in Las Vegas. We were back in the hunt.

I searched the Internet using the term "Clark County Nevada Marriage License" that took me right to the Clark County Recorder's Office online search index. I searched Ross Murphy's name and found the marriage between Ross and Cheryl. But guess what? I found no divorce. Big surprise, huh? So I searched a little more and—are you sitting down?— I found another marriage for Ross in Las Vegas about ten years before his marriage to Cheryl. Any divorce? Nope. Some men just don't change. He liked to get married on his binges in Las Vegas, but I guess somehow it never occurred to him that maybe he ought to get divorced once in a while.

So what did Laurel end up doing? She confronted Ross. He initially denied that he was still married. Then he admitted he and Cheryl were still married but denied any previous marriage. Eventually, yes, he admitted to both marriages and no divorces. Laurel is undecided whether to continue seeing him or not. At least she has the facts and knows that if the relationship continues there is no marriage in their immediate future—unless they take a trip to Vegas.

THE SHORT LIST

♦ **Search Civil records** in the county where you think the divorce occurred.

♦ **Search the "County Recorder's Office" or the "Official Records"** where the divorce most probably occurred.

♦ **Search property records** where the marital home may be to see if the property is still in both the husband's and wife's name. If so, there's a good likelihood that he's not divorced.

♦ To **find the county records**, use an Internet search for Clerk of the Court or County Recorder's Office.

♦ **Find the county records** using (http://www.brbpublications.com/).

♦ **When making pretext calls**, consider spoofing your caller ID.

♦ When all else fails, **get the boyfriend drunk** and drag a little more information out of him.

CHAPTER 4

WHERE DO YOU FIND CRIMINAL RECORDS?

I met Judith Shelf, a 40-year-old widow, two years ago. She had two children: a fifteen-year-old daughter and a ten-year-old son. Her husband died from a sudden onset of pancreatic cancer six months prior to our meeting. Three months after diagnosis he was dead. She and her husband had worked fulltime for one of the nation's largest banks.

For six months she hadn't even thought about dating or men or anything other than her children and her work. Her husband had several substantial life insurance policies so the first thing she did was pay off her modest home and bank the rest of the money in conservative money market savings accounts.

But now she recognized she had needs and desires. She was still young and wanted to live a full life. One Sunday at church she was introduced to Burt, who was forty-five, dressed well, and was reasonably well spoken. He'd taken her to dinner a few times and he clearly wanted a more serious relationship. She thought his table manners were "less than stellar," but she wasn't from high society herself. Still, something seemed "off" to her about him. He drank, she thought, a little too heavily when they went out, although he never passed out on her couch.

Did she want to introduce this man into her family? She had a son and a teenage daughter. Maybe she shouldn't date until her children were off to college and out of the home. But did life require her to trudge a solitary journey for the next ten years? If she did that, she worried that at fifty nobody would want her.

All of those thoughts whirled around in Judith's mind. Her physical desires were strong but the desire to protect her children was, of course, stronger. The loneliness she felt at night, after the children went to bed and she lay there by herself, crying at times for the loss of her husband, the unfairness of her situation, were she feared, going to push her into a deep whirlpool of depression. Didn't she deserve to have a life of her own?

"Steve," she said, "I need to know more about Burt. He seems nice enough, but . . ." and she explained her situation to me.

I could see her vulnerability and how she would appeal to someone less than scrupulous. She had money in the bank, a free and clear roof over her head, and a good job. These parts of her life she shouldn't have revealed to the new man in her life until she knew him better. It was a perfect situation for any freeloader. She told me she'd gone back to the gym, dropped a few pounds, and bought some new clothes. She made an attractive target and was physically attractive.

"What's his date of birth?" I asked. She had no idea. So I told her to write down the number on his license plate and call me with it when she had it.

The criminal justice system records key mostly off name and date of birth, not a person's social security number, as many people believe. Take "Steven Brown" again. In almost every jurisdiction where I search criminal records I usually first search my own name to make sure I'm searching the correct databases. I use "Steven Brown" as a test name because such a common name seems to have felony records everywhere.

In order to search for criminal records and to be sure that you have the right person's records you need first and last name and date of birth. Race, sex, middle name, and any other identifiers will help in determining that you're looking at the right record. If you're not sure that the person you are dating has told you his real name, then you should probably just move on to someone else.

If you're searching criminal records on a female who has been married, maybe multiple times, then you'll need to conduct the search with all of her names—maiden and married.

THE TRUTH ABOUT NATIONAL CRIMINAL SEARCHES

There is only one real national criminal record search. Don't be fooled by some of the "pay databases" which advertise online that for

$24.95 they can conduct a national criminal search on your subject. It just isn't true.

The one real national criminal record search is a search of the automated criminal history record information (also known as the Interstate Identification Index) which is accessed through the same network as the National Crime Information Center (NCIC), a database run by the FBI and available only to law enforcement. There are some exceptions. If, for instance, you provide a set of scanned fingerprints to the FBI for certain jobs, like FDIC insured banks, then yes, a search of their records will be completed.

So just what exactly are you purchasing for $24.95 from these Internet background check companies? Let's look at the price first. If you Google NCIC, the first company that appears claims it conducts NCIC searches. It states "View anyone's criminal history & search criminals in seconds." So you input the name and the state of the person you want to search and, of course, they then want you to set up a user ID and a password. Next they'll ask for your credit card and the card's billing address before you can continue. They may offer a trial membership that you can cancel within three days. After that they'll bill you for six months in advance and will continue to bill you automatically every six months for $89.16. All this for a search you can conduct for yourself, for free, all of sudden ends up costing you close to $200.

Another company that advertises for $12.95 claims that their search includes all 50 states, Puerto Rico, and Washington, D.C. "Our reports contain all arrests and convictions, including the type and nature of the arrest, court dates, and final disposition, including parole, probation, and incarceration records." Sounds good, doesn't it? It just isn't true; don't buy into it.

Judith continued to see Burt for the next few days and asked me why I didn't just use one of these online criminal record sites to check him out instead of jumping through the hoops, searching his vehicle license plate to get his date of birth, and running the social security trace to see where he lived in the past.

I explained to her what these "online criminal search databases" really sold. As an example, I contacted the "$12.95 national criminal check" people and asked for a list of their coverage area. They refused to provide it. However, what most of these folks are selling is a search of the sexual offender registries from each state, a search of the department of corrections database from most of the states (but not all), and then some state and local county government databases that include arrest and conviction information. Sounds good? Well, don't be fooled. Unless your man spent time in a state penitentiary, it's unlikely he'll show up—even if he spent six months in the county jail. To be fair, some of these databases include records from various states' Administrator of Court (AOC) files. Some states provide a database collected from the state AOC and the criminal record information is reasonably current. Many states still provide data from their AOC but the information may not have been updated in years.

These "online criminal pay databases" are selling data of arrests and convictions from five counties in the state of Florida. Fine, but Florida has sixty-seven counties. So if the guy you're interested in works in Duval County but lives in the suburbs next door in St. Johns County and was arrested at his home, this database won't show the charges against him in

St. Johns, County. Don't waste your money. I can't tell you how many clients have come to me after spending several hundred dollars on these "Internet criminal background search" sites and have nothing to show for their money.

CONDUCTING THE CRIMINAL BACKGROUND SEARCH

The general rule in conducting a criminal background search is to search the best available records. Aren't all records the same? No, they're not. In Florida you can search criminal records at the Florida Department of Law Enforcement (FDLE) www.fdle.state.fl.us for $24. Is that the best available search? Not really, not terrible, just not all-inclusive. For instance, Judith's new boyfriend, Burt, was arrested for Driving Under the Influence (DUI), but the charge was reduced to reckless driving. His record won't show at the FDLE site, yet you can be sure that Judith would like to know about it. If he had been arrested for armed robbery, then yes, FDLE would have that charge in their database.

Where are the best available records? Generally the best available records are considered to be those at the county courthouse where the person was charged. Many of the more than 3,500 counties in the United States have their criminal records online and can be viewed for free. The question then arises, How do you know which counties to search? There are 67 counties in Florida. Where do you look? It's not really feasible to search in all 3,500 counties in the United States.

My company provides a social security trace, which takes the person's social security number and runs it through various databases using an algorithm that shows us where the subject has resided over the last ten years or so. Then we search the criminal records in those counties.

You won't be able to do a social security trace yourself. However, with some careful and subtle questioning, you can find out where your potential boyfriend has lived for the last ten years. And that's free. Suppose he tells you he lived in Jacksonville, Florida; Phoenix, Arizona, and Grand Junction, Colorado. What do you do next?

Go to www.5ThingsWomenNeedToKnow.com. If you wish, give us the go ahead and we will do the work for you. Or you can search all of the free sites for yourself to your heart's content. If he lives or lived in a county that is not online for free, you can place an order and for a small fee someone will go to that courthouse, search the criminal records in that county and we'll let you know what we find.

Check Arizona and you'll see that you can search 153 courts out of 180 courts at the Arizona Judicial Branch website. These courts include Justice of the Peace courts, Municipal Courts, and Superior Courts.

If your new boyfriend lived in Colorado you can search the entire state at one site for $5 at www.CoCourts.com and for $2 dollars more you'll get Denver County, which has its own site and costs $2 per search. Or you can have us search it and the other places he's lived for you but it will cost you a bit more at www.5ThingsWomenNeedToKnow.com.

States like New York you can't search yourself. They have a good statewide search, but you have to subscribe. The cost to search New York is $65 **per name**. There is no way to do a county search in New York but we can do the state that wide search for you.

Do you want to see any criminal charges your boyfriend who lived Jacksonville, Florida, might have? Our website will lead you to the Duval County site which is totally free. Be sure and search any surrounding counties as well.

We ran the social security trace on Burt and for the last twenty years he's lived in Duval County, Florida. We searched the county records, and, yep, found three DUIs for him. Not good news for Judith. But we also found several domestic violence complaints against him from a former wife, and two aggravated battery charges that were reduced to misdemeanor battery. He pled Nolo Contendre to the battery charges and received an Adjudication of Guilt Withheld disposition.

"Nolo Contendre"

Nolo Contendre *is a plea available in some states that means the subject of the complaint is not pleading innocent or guilty. Instead he/she is "not contesting" the charges.*

"Adjudication of Guilt Withheld"

Adjudication of Guilt Withheld *is a disposition given in a criminal case which allows the defendant to honestly say he was not convicted. It does not mean he is innocent, just that the adjudication of guilt was withheld. Nevertheless, usually the arrest for that charge will still appear when a background search is conducted.*

Judith decided she didn't want Burt around her children and certainly wouldn't trust him to drive them to school. And she couldn't allow someone with violent tendencies in her life or around the kids, so she dumped him and moved on.

THE SHORT LIST

♦ **Determine your subject's full name and date of birth.** Criminal Justice system records key off of name and date of birth.

♦ **Ask a lot of questions.** Find out where he's lived for the last ten years.

♦ **Do not pay** for "online background searches."

♦ **Search the best available records** which are usually (but not always) county-level searches.

♦ **Don't get confused.** Go to www.5ThingsWomenNeedToKnow.com and we'll do it for you.

♦ **Send us** to the county courthouse to conduct the search for you for a small fee if a free county search is not available.

CHAPTER 5

THE INTERNET

DATING SCAMS AND CATFISHING

Judith Shelf, from Chapter 4 decided Burt wasn't right for her family since he clearly had a drinking issue. She'd met Burt at church and if she couldn't find a good man at church where could she find one? She wasn't a big drinker herself and sitting around bars getting picked up wasn't her idea of a good time, so she went to the Internet. There are dozens of dating sites on the Internet. There she could read a man's profile, see his photograph, and decide from the privacy of her home whether she was the least bit interested in the face staring back at her on the screen.

JUDITH'S STORY

She responded to several men's profiles and was pretty quickly Instant Messaging one fellow in particular, Robert, who said he lived in

Nashville, Tennessee. He had a cell phone number that began with the area code used in Nashville and they seemed to have a lot in common. Although he had a phone, all of their communication was via Instant Messaging.

Judith and Robert spent several hours a night Instant Messaging each other for the first week. During the second week Robert called Judith and said he might not be near a computer for the next couple of days because his eleven-year-old son had been hit by a car and was in the hospital. He was embarrassed to ask but because he had no health insurance and he had to make some kind of good faith payment to the hospital, he wondered if she could send him five hundred dollars by Western Union.

Judith, with two teenagers of her own, was sympathetic and said she'd be glad to loan him the $500. He was ecstatic and asked her to wire it, but to put another man's name on the Western Union instructions. This request gave her some concern but she had a good job, a paid off house, and life insurance proceeds in the bank from a recently deceased husband, so $500 was not a big investment in what she hoped might be a lifetime relationship.

What was the reason the money had to go to someone else's name and address? Well, Robert said he lost his billfold a few days ago and didn't have any identification of his own at that moment, but this other fellow was a good friend of his and would go to Western Union, get the money, and give it to him. Riiiight.

She sent the money to Tennessee. He called her when he got the money and was very grateful. You can probably guess what came next. Two days later he was back on the computer, Instant Messaging Judith. Now his son was released from the hospital but needed to see an orthopedic surgeon for some procedure that was going to cost $2,500. Could Judith loan him the money until he got back on his feet? He'd lost his job the month before. He promised to pay her back.

That's when Judith called me again.

"Steve, I really like this guy, but I'm not dumb. Well, not that dumb. Can you check him out for me?"

She gave me the contact info she had for Robert, who was forty years old, and the name and address of the fellow that she'd sent the money to.

It didn't take me very long, maybe a half-hour of database searching, to figure out that Robert didn't exist. Another few minutes and we had the "money man" identified as a sixty-year-old guy who didn't live at the address he gave but lived next door to it. Plus he had arrest records that went back ten years for various frauds. At least he didn't have any arrests for violent crimes. But it gets better.

A few months after the hospital scam, Judith received an email from Nigeria, saying that this "police official" had recovered a laptop from a known scammer and he found her contact information in the computer. The police had allegedly arrested "Robert" whose real name was Joseph, and wanted the details of how "Joseph" had scammed her.

Judith, being the trusting person she was, told this "police official" the whole story. "Was Robert/Joseph in jail?" Judith asked.

"No, while he was under arrest he escaped." But the police official would be willing to send her a copy of "Joseph's" police file, if she were interested. There would be a slight copying and mailing fee. "About two hundred and fifty dollars," the policeman said. Up until recently this "police official" contacted Judith every couple of months.

It's not at all unusual for the victim in a scam like Judith's to be re-contacted. This is called "follow-up scamming." Since the victim has been scammed once, she/he is more likely to fall for another scam than some random person. To quote from *Wikipedia*, "Often after a scam, the victim is contacted again by the scammer, representing himself as a law enforcement officer."

The scam on Judith is classic Nigerian. First the person, in this case, "Robert," is not real. Second, their communication is either via cell phone or Instant Messaging. Third, some sudden tragedy/accident/misfortune strikes and money is needed right way. Fourth, the money must be sent via Western Union or Moneygram, (the transaction, once completed, is irreversible, cannot be traced, and the money can never be recovered). Fifth, the victim is contacted again, this time by law enforcement and more money is requested.

It gets better still with Judith's story. In the process of putting this book together, I spoke to her to see if there had been any follow-up from Nigeria. Joseph actually "contacted me as himself." She is still so naïve. This is what she said: "Apparently he has changed his life around and is contacting people to say he is sorry. He came on a Webcam and talked to me for a bit."

I asked her for more details. Joseph was a black, native-born Nigerian, living in Nigeria. All of his Instant Messaging was done from Nigeria. "He said he liked me and felt bad and would like to continue to talk."

Steven Kerry Brown

"He wanted to be friends," she said. "He was not real happy with my answer or comments." Finally she wised up and cussed him out.

A great many frauds are committed every day through the Internet. There is probably not a person who has an email address that hasn't received a Nigerian scam email.

So how can you be sure that the man you're talking to, Instant Messaging, or otherwise communicating with is actually who he says he is?

Because I wrote *The Complete Idiot's Guide to Private Investigating*, I get phone calls and emails from across the country asking for advice. "How can I find this?" Or, "Where do I search to find my former sweetheart?" My next book will be on *Finding Lost Loves, Biological Relatives, and Deadbeat Parents*.

MEN TAKE THE BAIT TOO

KEVIN'S STORY

It is not just women who are targeted for scams. Men are in the bull's eye just as often.

A while ago, Kevin from southern California sent me an email:

"Hi Steven, I hope that you could please help out. I lent someone allot [sic]) of money and now they refuse to pay it back. I did a reverse phone number search. I used the Argali home edition [phone and address search site— http://www.argali.com/] like it says in your book

43

but no luck. Any ideas on how to find this person would be very much appreciated."

What is Kevin's story? He met Jill on an Internet dating site. She said she lived in southern California too but I traced her purported phone number to an address in San Francisco. That didn't really prove where she was or where she was from or even if she was really a female. She said she was originally from Mexico. Both parents and her older sister were killed in an automobile accident. She said she was about thirty-five years old. She had lost her husband five years ago. She traveled a lot and right then was on a business trip to Sweden.

Jill sent Kevin two photos of herself. She looks about nineteen. She also sent him some semi-erotic emails saying she was a "G-string type of lady. I love the bikini swim suit." Over the space of ten days she convinced him to send $8,500 in three installments of $2,500, $2,500 and $3,500 via Western Union to some man in New York allegedly to be used to pay custom's taxes on antiques and artwork that she was importing. She said she ran an antique business and was scouring Sweden for antiques for her store.

Where was her antique store located? Good question. It's one question that Kevin forgot to ask. Jill did and still does have a Linked-In page. If you're not familiar with www.Linkedin.com, it's a business referral page for "professionals." On her Linkedin page she has only one "connection." Jill also now has a Facebook page, but under a different Hispanic name.

Kevin told me, "I'm unemployed right now and living off my Navy retirement and VA benefits. If I don't find her in the next month my house will go into foreclosure." What he meant was that if he didn't get his money back in the next month, his house would go into foreclosure.

Jill ceased all communication with him as soon as the last installment of the money arrived in New York. Big surprise there, huh? Her page still is up on Linkedin and Facebook. I suspect she is out there still scamming love-sick horny guys. Actually I suspect she is a he and resides in Nigeria. If she/he talked to him on the phone, how did he disguise his voice? Well, look at the next section that deals with the Manti Te'o debacle.

In putting this book together I contacted Kevin again. This time he finally confessed that it wasn't $8,500 that he sent her. It was over $30,000. I think he was embarrassed in the beginning to tell me how much money he was out.

The above amounts are not huge but $30,000 is substantial. I have a colleague who had a wealthy client in Singapore that was taken for $1.3 million from a man who claimed to reside in Great Britain. When he was finally tracked down, you guessed it—he was in Nigeria.

A woman in Orem, Utah, was scammed for $200,000 from a man who claimed he was British. She sent various amounts to him ranging from $5,000 to $10,000 at a time. This relationship began on an online dating site aimed at religious singles.

CatFishing

Catfish is a 2010 American documentary film, directed by Henry Joost and Ariel Schulman, involving a young man being filmed by his brother and friend as he builds a romantic relationship with a young woman on the social networking website Facebook. In the documentary the young woman proves to not only **not** be who she says she is, but has fifteen different Facebook profiles. Catfishing is using the Internet's social media or communications to lure someone into a relationship when the lure is just bait and not reality.

MANTI TE'O

Manti Te'o is the Notre Dame football star that carried on a relationship with a girl supposedly named Lennay Kekua. Te'o "met" Kekua online and they maintained a relationship for over two years. He talked to "her" on the phone, tweeted her, and texted her. "She" left him voice mails on his phone. If you listen to the voice mails they do sound feminine. All during this time, they never used Skype or any other webcam service where Te'o would have learned that Kekua, was not a female, but was in fact a male named Ronaiah Tuiasosopo.

Tuiasosopo recently appeared on the Dr. Phil television show. There he admitted that he was actually the voice behind Kekua. He said he was confused and didn't know if he was gay or not. He'd been sexually molested and raped since he was twelve years old. He didn't name the person who'd abused him but it sounded as if it were a friend of his father's rather than a family member.

Dr. Phil didn't believe that Tuiasosopo could have left those feminine sounding voice mails. He sent copies of the voice mails to three different audio forensic specialists to compare them to the tapes of the Dr.

46

Phil interview. All three said it was unlikely that the voices were made by the same person. Finally he had one of his producers go to Tuiasosopo's home and in his bedroom Tuiasosopo read the transcripts of the voice mails in a feminine voice. This time all three audio forensics experts agreed that they were almost 100% certain that Tuiasosopo left those voice mail recordings on Manti Te'o's cell phone. Just because someone sounds like a woman or a man, it doesn't mean they are one or the other.

Because someone speaks with no accent, British, South African, Hispanic, New York, or southern United States you can't be sure who you are speaking to.

Sounds kind of like Judith Shelf, doesn't it? At least the fake Robert and the real scammer, Joseph, were males. Was Kevin's Jill really a female? We'll never know. But we do know that his $30,000 is long gone. He has just recently been contacting me about attempting to track her down and get her identified so that he can sue her or him, perhaps? Take note of the points below and avoid falling prey to these Internet scammers.

THE SHORT LIST

♦ **Never just Instant Message.** Insist that the person you contact has a webcam and use Yahoo Messenger, Skype, FaceTime, or some other webcam service. With a webcam at least you'll know that Jill is not really Joseph.

♦ **If your new beau doesn't have a webcam, offer to send him/her one.** If he wants you to send him the money to buy one, beware. If you don't send the money and insist on you sending him the webcam, scammers will typically become upset and throw a tantrum. They don't want to talk to you via webcam because then you'll see that Jill really is Joe.

♦ **Be wary if some sudden tragedy or accident strikes and he needs money right away.** This is a very typical ploy of scammers. It can be an accident, a kidnapping, loss of passport and currency, or any other emergency.

♦ **Don't send any money to someone you have not had a face-to-face meeting with.** Most people are good natured and charitable. These are traits scammers prey upon.

♦ **Don't send money via Western Union or MoneyGram.** If they won't take a check, a wire transfer to their bank account, or a cashier's check, then don't send money. Insist on this. Chances are it'll be the last time this person ever contacts you.

♦ **Get some specifics about their background.** Something you can verify yourself. Jill's Linkedin page said she graduated from Ryerson University in Canada. Call the alumni association or the registrar and see if she indeed graduated.

♦ **Be careful with online dating sites.** Don't let your hormones or emotions outweigh your common sense.

CHAPTER 6

DOES HE HAVE ANY MONEY?

One question you need to get the answer to is if the man you're dating is poor or rich. Is he struggling financially or does he have money in the bank? I know this may sound Machiavellian, but "Steve," you say, "there are many fine, good-hearted men that make terrific husbands and don't have a lot of money." I agree and I don't necessarily recommend basing your romantic interest in a person on the size of their net worth. But you should be aware of the person's general financial status and his ability to handle money before you become too enamored. No, I'm not suggesting you become a gold digger. But don't be stupid, either.

I was traveling on a plane a while back and I noted that a young stewardess had a pin on her uniform—not her name-tag—that had the logo and name of a large textile manufacturer. The company still bears the name of the man who invented that particular type of clothing.

I also noted she wore a pretty fair-sized diamond engagement ring on her left hand. So I asked her why she was wearing that pin. Were the airline's uniforms now made out of that type of material?

"No," she replied. "I decided when I was in college that it was just as easy to fall in love with someone who was rich as someone who was poor." So she spent as much time as she could hanging around Martha's Vineyard—an island off the coast of Massachusetts well known as the "playground" of the rich and famous. Sure enough it worked for her. She fell in love with the son of the man who'd invented that fabric. Their wedding date was three months off. As a side note, I gave that advice to both of my daughters but, of course, neither of them paid heed.

You can't legally run a credit check in the United States on a prospective date to see his credit standing, though you can in other countries. So what to do? Keep reading.

DEBORAH'S STORY

Deborah had been dating Ralph who seemed very nice. She liked him but she had some questions about him. In the four weeks she'd been dating him he'd never invited her over to his place. He worked as a bartender in an upscale establishment and drove a reasonably nice car. It wasn't a BMW or a Lexus, or some other high end model, but it had four tires and a motor that started. She did recognize that many frugal people drove their cars until they gave out. She admired frugality.

Ralph apparently enjoyed playing golf and gave her a new golf bag and set of women's clubs. Not an inexpensive gift. She knew that as a bartender he couldn't be making huge wages but Ralph said the tips where he worked were excellent. Deborah wanted to know more about Ralph before she became too emotionally invested in him.

The fact that he was a bartender made me curious. Very often bartender jobs draw people who like to drink. The first thing we did was run a driving history on Ralph. Yep, he had two DUIs. In my book, unless he was now sober and a recovering alcoholic, two DUIs would disqualify him as a potential mate. Next we searched civil records. We found two collection suits filed against him for non-payment of loans—another red flag.

Probably one of the best ways to determine if a person is financially stable is a search of county property records. Does the person own a home? Is it in foreclosure? Is there equity in the home or was it purchased with no money down?

In Ralph's case we found his address from his driver's license. We could not find any records of real property he owned in the county where he lived. We looked at the tax and ownership records for his address and discovered that the property was in his mother's name. A drive-by of the residence showed that one of the vehicles parked there was registered to Ralph and the other to his mother. Yep. Ralph, age forty-two, lived with his mom, in her house. This explained why he hadn't invited Deborah to his place.

Now, there are lots of reasons why your mother may be living with you. She might be ill and you might be taking care of her. You might have sold your place and moved in with her to do that. So we searched the official records at the county clerk's office. Remember, we talked about how to do that in Chapter Three. The "Official Records" are the records recorded in the Clerk of the Court's office or at the County Recorder's

Office. (It may be called something different in your state.) These records usually have a book and page number.

When we searched for Ralph's name we found no record of his ever having owned a home, a condo, or any other piece of real property. Yep, he was living with his mom because that was the best he could do. You won't have access to bank account information but you can probably guess that Ralph wouldn't have much in his bank account. Later, Deborah discovered that the golf bag and clubs had been given back to him by an old girlfriend he had bought them for. She gave them back to him when they broke up. Deborah didn't play golf but she kept the clubs anyway and later sold them on Craig's List.

IS THERE EQUITY IN HIS PROPERTY?

Joan was dating Kenneth. He took her to his condo one evening and cooked dinner. The condo was reasonably nice in what she thought was an "upscale" waterfront complex. He told her he'd been living there for only a few months. She called me and wanted to know what the scoop was on this guy.

I suggested that she go online at the property appraiser's website for the county and check those records. The property was in his name. In her county, the property appraiser's website actually had sales records and told her how much Kenneth paid for the property and what the sales history was. It also told her what the current assessed full market value was.

Now, some states don't assess real property at full market value so the figure you see there may be some percentage of the real market value. A call to the property appraiser will clear that up for you if you're not sure.

Why do you care? You'll want to have some idea of the property's value for the next step.

If your county property appraiser's website doesn't give you any clue as to the property's value, you can try going to http://www.zillow.com. On that website's home page, type in the property address and you'll probably find an estimated value for the property. You might also find sales information for it, the number of bedrooms and baths, and the square footage. There is no exact value to a home. A piece of real property is worth what someone is willing to pay for it. That's okay. We don't need an exact value; an approximation will do.

Next, Joan went to the official records, as we discussed above and in Chapter Three. She found the mortgage recorded when Kenneth purchased the property sixteen years ago. That gave her pause because he said he'd only been in the place for four months.

The records show he'd placed a first mortgage on the condo for $84,000. She also found the deed given to Kenneth from the sellers of the condo. While the deed itself showed no price, the county clerk's website showed a "consideration value" of $93,000. This meant that Kenneth put about $9,000 down on the property, not counting recording costs and other fees. But all of this occurred, about sixteen years ago. Joan was perplexed.

I did some more digging and Kenneth appeared to be one shrewd guy. He did in fact buy that condo when it was in foreclosure by what was then First Union Bank from the previous owner for $93,000. He sold that condo eight years later for $176,000. In 2007 at the height of the housing market boom, that person sold the condo for $389,000. Then the market crashed and the condo was foreclosed on again. Once more Kenneth bought the foreclosed condo in 2011, this time for $148,000. The property appraiser now has it assessed for a fair market value of $152,250. Good for Kenneth and good for Joan. She'd found herself someone who had some pretty good sense when it came to real estate.

One more little item about Kenneth and this condo: We looked up the current mortgage on the condo. He'd placed a mortgage on it for $110,000, which meant that he had $40,000 in equity in the property. Kenneth looks a lot better than some guy who's living with his mother.

THE NEW GUY AND THE GREAT CAR

So the new guy in your life drives a BMW. Doesn't that mean he's got money? Not really. What if he's driving a new Aston Martin? Well, yeah, it probably means he has money. Still, you should do your research. The car could be leased. It could belong to his mom and she just lets him borrow it. What research? I'll show you.

You probably won't be able to tell how much he paid for the car, but you want to see if there's a lien on it. If he's driving a car that's ten years old and there's a lien on it, then you'll want to throw that fact into your equation after you do the property research. If he's driving a new car, and it's in his name (not a lease or company vehicle) and there is no lien, then when he purchased the vehicle he probably paid cash. If it's a four- or five-year old car and there's no lien, he's probably paid it off. Good for him.

About half of the states make the automobile registration information fairly easy to obtain. In these states the information is not public but it is available to private investigators.

The reason this information is not public is because of the Driver's Privacy Protection Act (DPPA). The DPPA is an act that was passed in the U.S. Congress because of a murder that took place in California.

Let me quote from my book, *The Complete Idiot's Guide to Private Investigating*:

> In 1989, Robert John Bardo hired a private investigator to get the home address of actress Rebecca Schaffer, who at that time played on the television sitcom *My Sister Sam*. The P.I. got the information from the California Department of Motor Vehicles and sold it to Bardo. Schaffer was expecting Francis Ford Coppola to come to her door and discuss an audition for his film, *Godfather III*. When the bell rang, Schaffer opened the door and found Bardo there instead. She asked him to leave and closed the door. Bardo went away but returned very upset. He rang again but hid so that Schaffer had to step out of the apartment to see who was there. Bardo shot her once in the chest and fled.
>
> As a result of this incident, the U.S. Congress passed the Driver's Privacy Protection Act. This act prohibits the release of information pertaining to driver's licenses, but included fourteen specific exemptions. Licensed private investigators are listed as exception number eight, as long as the information is used for one of the other thirteen reasons.

The bottom line is, you can no longer walk up to your local DMV and request this information.

If you know someone in the car business, used or new, that person can probably find out if there's a lien on the car. If you don't, you might try your local private investigator or give us a call. It shouldn't cost you more $30 to $50 to get this information, if it's available in your state.

THE SHORT LIST

♦ **There is nothing wrong with making sure the guy you're dating is financially stable.** How to handle money is an important trait in the person you're going to bring into your life. Conjugal life is easier if it's not marred with arguments over money.

♦ **If the man you're considering lives with his parents, he may not be the right one.** If his parents live with him because of age or health, that's a different story.

♦ **Check property records to see if he owns his own home/condo.** The property appraiser's website will usually tell you the value of the residence and who pays the taxes on that property.

♦ **Search the Clerk of the Court's records or the County Recorder's Office.** The "Official Records" will have copies of the mortgages and deeds on real property that the new boyfriend owns. They will show you the amount of any mortgages on the property. Look for first mortgages and second and even third mortgages. A "satisfaction" is filed if the first mortgage is paid off and the house is refinanced for more money or with better terms.

♦ **Determine the value of the residence.** This can be done by using the assessed valuation of the property which you'll find at the property appraiser's office, or you can use www.zillow.com for an approximation.

♦ **Is there equity in the property?** Subtract the amount of the mortgage from the fair market value of the property and you can determine the approximate amount of equity in the property.

♦ **Determine if there is a lien on the car he drives.** You'll probably need a friend in the auto business or to hire a private investigator to determine this.

CHAPTER 7

DRUG AND ALCOHOL ADDICTIONS?

In the last part of Chapter One, I mentioned Amy. Let's see what we can learn from her story.

Amy was in her very early forties and had never married. She had a professional job in the healthcare field making almost $200,000 a year. One night she and her brother stopped after midnight at a bar to have a few drinks. If you're a woman, nothing really good happens at a bar after midnight. But Amy was with her brother and things were fine.

They both noticed a group of women sitting at the bar with them. After a couple of martinis Amy asked her brother if he was ready to have her "twist his head." He didn't have a clue as to what she was talking about.

She told him that the women next to them were lesbians.

"Nah," he said. He couldn't believe it.

"Watch," she said.

Before he knew it Amy was making out with a woman who was the mother of one of those girls who was about Amy's age, early forties. The mother of the lesbian girl was not gay and if you believe her, neither is Amy. Amy just "likes to kiss chicks." Amy says that just because she likes to kiss girls that "doesn't make her gay, bi, or anything."

In a minute her brother had a gorgeous guy standing right beside him. His name was Jack. He was all smiles. He asked her brother who was the hot "bitch" in the blue dress with the blue eyes.

"That's my sister," he said,

"Oops, sorry, man."

"Nah, that's okay. Go up and introduce yourself to her. She's cool."

Amy and Jack sat next to each other.

After a few minutes of conversation and another drink Amy grabbed Jack's penis "to see what he had." She figured she had nothing to lose and would probably never see Jack again. Although Jack didn't realize it, Amy remembered going to high school with him. He was one of the "untouchables" in high school—very good looking, very popular, and a few years ahead of her in school.

She gave him her phone number. The following weekend was the Fourth of July. He lived in St. Augustine, Florida, about forty miles south of where she lived. There was going to be a party in Vilano Beach and Jack asked her if she'd like to go with him. She accepted.

The next Friday after work, she went home, changed clothes, and drove down to his place. They left Jack's and drove to the party at a friend's house. This was their first date. They hadn't been at the party very long when he pulled Amy into the bathroom and laid out some cocaine. She had tried cocaine only once when she was twenty. She had to ask him what to do with it. Now she realizes she should have turned around and not looked back at the first moment when Jack produced the coke.

Every time they were together, the third player was always present: cocaine. Amy had a professional license in the medical field "that I worked my ass off to get." Now she realized her behavior was putting her license in jeopardy. Her job also required random drug testing—a big concern for her. She ran these concerns by Jack and he always had the perfect answer for all of them. He told her that if she ever had to go for drug testing she was to call or text him and he would make sure that he got her some clean urine for the test. That seemed like an unlikely and complicated scenario.

Jack's family loved Amy. And why wouldn't they? She'd never been married. She had a good job, was well dressed, and drove a Mercedes. Jack's parents thought that finally their wayward son was hooking up with a good girl. Most of their dates were on Jack's turf in St. Augustine. In the seven months they were together Jack had been inside Amy's condo only three or four times.

Always being on his turf with his friends should have been a red flag for Amy. In hindsight she also realized that spending all of their time with his friends was a problem. It just didn't occur to her at the time. And why were they always with his friends? Because all of his friends also did coke and her friends didn't do drugs. She realized that she didn't really want to party with her friends and Jack because she didn't want her friends to know she was doing cocaine. She felt she had way too much to lose and especially didn't want her family to know.

They dated from July 4th to Christmas Eve. On Christmas Eve he proposed to her. He gave her a beautiful two-carat marquee ring. Jack's family was floored that finally their son was really going to get married and settle down. Jack, of course, wanted Amy to move in with him in St. Augustine. Where she currently lived was a five-minute drive to where she worked. The drive from St. Augustine would have been almost an hour. It made no difference to Jack. He wanted her with him all the time. He didn't care that she had a very stable, regimented job and life.

She recognizes now that her work was beginning to deteriorate. Co-workers were noticing a difference in her behavior. Her boss even called her in one day to chat with her and asked if she liked her job. At the time she didn't understand why he would ask her that. But now with a clear vision of what was going on she can see what her boss and co-workers saw. She was always tired and frequently late to work.

For the seven months they were together she would come home from work on Friday, pack her duffle bag, change the kitty litter, put out the cat food, drive down to St. Augustine, and start partying until Sunday evening. Sunday night she would drive home and begin the week all over again. She spent the work weekdays recuperating from the weekend.

One day she realized the position she was in. Their entire relationship was built on cocaine. She began to push back from the cocaine. When Jack offered it she would not take it, but he snorted it anyway. About 11:00 P.M. he was ready to go bar hopping. She would go home and go to bed. Jack never stayed during the week when Amy was in Jacksonville working. He was a total partier, out every night at different bars and restaurants.

One weekend she couldn't find Jack. Her cousin and friends were in town. They decided to go to a biker bar in St. Augustine. They also went to Jack's place. He wasn't there. She called him and he said he was in Palatka at a friend's party. The breakup began the next day.

He called her and left three very angry messages on her home phone. The first message told her that he thought she was wonderful. "The sex is great but I'm tired of being verbally abused by you. I came by your place and took the ring back. Things aren't going to work out for us and I'm tired of being bashed by you."

On that particular Sunday afternoon, she had gone to the condo swimming pool for about an hour and had left the ring on the counter and her front door unlocked. During that hour Jack sneaked in and took the ring—valued at $21,000—and left.

She drove down to St. Augustine to confront him but he wasn't home. She waited for him. When he finally arrived, she noticed that he would not take his sunglasses off. Was he doing some other drugs besides cocaine? Amy asked for the ring back and eventually he gave it to her. She didn't wear the ring because the engagement was off, but kept hiding it in different places in case he came over and tried to steal it again.

About two months later, late one night she began receiving texts from Jack. At two-thirty in the morning she received a text saying he would be at her place in thirty minutes. He showed up at her door, his face unshaven, smelling horrible, and looking like crap. He looked as though he lived on the street. She immediately took him in, thinking that maybe there was a small chance they could salvage the relationship. She put the ring back on her finger so Jack would think she'd been wearing it the whole time.

She tried to get him to lie down and get some sleep but he refused. He asked her to go put on an "outfit." He had purchased some negligees for her that he particularly liked. She stood by the bed wearing a negligee and high heels and Jack came up the stairs. He grabbed both of her hands with one of his hands. As if in slow motion he slid the ring right off her hand and immediately fled her condo. She'd never seen him move as fast as he ran out the front door with her ring.

The next day she called the police and filed a report. Though Jack was not arrested for the theft of the ring, she hired an attorney and filed a civil suit against him. Legally the engagement ring belongs to her, as it was a gift from Jack. She doesn't really want the ring back, but wants to hurt him where it'll hurt the most—his wallet. She suspects he may have needed the ring to pay off some drug debts. She figures she spent $25,000 on Jack's drugs during the time they were together. She almost lost her job, family, reputation, dignity, and respect for herself.

She realizes that she was a consenting adult and that she chose to use the cocaine. That was her mistake. She'd been bored and not dating anyone when she met Jack and wanted "something new." She wanted to shake up her life.

"Boy, did he shake up my life. It was like being whipped in a blender," she said.

Had she known that Jack had a record of trafficking in cocaine she never would have gone out with him. She says, "People are very manipulative and you can't be too careful. People can have you believing what they want you to believe, seeing what they want you to see. When do you really know them? They wine and dine you and tell you everything you want to hear."

Now Amy calls me when she meets some new guy and we do a little background on him before she goes out on a second or third date.

The red flag here, of course, was the first time Jack jerked her into that bathroom and offered the cocaine. Another flag was when Jack went to buy cocaine and asked her to finance it.

PRESCRIPTION DRUGS

Addiction to illegal and prescription drugs is a sure "keep away" sign. You probably won't realize the guy you're dating is actually addicted until you've seen him do the drugs on multiple occasions. Twice should be enough to make you realize that this person has a drug problem.

There are, of course, other addictions besides illegal drugs. Prescription drug addiction is as common as addiction to cocaine or crack cocaine. Hydrocodone, oxycodone, oxycotin, and Vicodin are probably the most addictive. In Chapter One I mentioned a family addicted to prescription drugs. The father and mother had both been in jail and their married son and daughter are currently in the state prison for the sale and distribution of illegally obtained prescription drugs. Xanax also known as alprazolam, and <u>lorazepam</u> (Ativan) are probably not as addictive as the previous list but one can become "dependent" upon them.

Red flags? If you're dating someone and you see that person take any of the above drugs two, three, or more times a day, there is a problem. Or if your date is riding as a passenger in your car and he falls asleep or passes out and he hasn't been drinking, then you need to consider that he might be addicted to a prescription drug. Is there a legitimate use for those drugs? Of course, there is. But if the drugs aren't prescribed by their own physician, watch out.

METHAMPHETAMINE

Then of course there is one drug we haven't mentioned. Methamphetamine, also known as "meth." I worked a case recently where a woman's daughter was living with the father of her child. She originally came to me because her daughter was going to move and not tell my client where she was going. My client, the grandmother, knew that this guy was no good. My client had rented a house for them to live in because neither the daughter nor the guy had a job. But finally the client had enough of their behavior and when the water was turned off for lack of payment, she refused to the pay the bill for them. The title and registration of my client's car that the two were driving was in my client's name.

So that she could maintain some contact with her grandchild she consented for me to put a GPS tracking device on the vehicle. The idea was to see where they moved to and let them work out their family problems. My client's granddaughter was twenty years old, her boyfriend, was twenty-two.

In watching the movements of the vehicle via the tracking device we were certain that he was either buying or selling drugs or both. He would drive around a three county area and make short stops at certain houses, over and over again, late at night and into the early morning. He also stopped at half a dozen different pharmacies during the day.

One of my investigators had a friend that was on the county sheriff's drug team so we spoke with him. He recognized some of the addresses as known drug sales sites and was interested in the case. I gave the deputy the Web address and login info so he could watch the vehicle himself. The plan was when he left a known drug house, a marked unit would pull him over and get permission to search the vehicle, or if the boyfriend was driving while impaired, they would arrest him and have my client come and retrieve her car.

One evening everything fell into place and all three of us, my client, the deputy, and I were watching his movements—the deputy from his office, my client from her home, and I from my office. About 1:00 A.M., the boyfriend drove into the next county and made one of his usual stops. The deputy called out the patrol units. They monitored his movements when he left the drug house in the other county. Once he crossed the county line into our county he was pulled over by a marked unit. The officer found drug paraphernalia on the seat next to him.

Possession of drug paraphernalia is a misdemeanor in Florida. They arrested him and my client retrieved her car. In the trunk were the raw ingredients needed to make meth.

They obtained a search warrant for the residence and found a full blown meth lab in the garage. The entire house was contaminated with meth. He was then charged with the manufacturing and distribution of methamphetamines. The sheriff's office had to call out the Hazmat team before they could go in and execute the search warrant.

My client's daughter saw the error in her choice of boyfriends. Think about it: their one-year-old child had been exposed to meth most of his life. Who knows what the long-term effects of that are going to be? My client and her daughter, and the grandchild are reunited. She wrote me:

Dear Steve,

A letter cannot begin to express my gratitude to you for all you did for my family! Without your help and dedication to this case none of it would have happened. I will be forever grateful to you for everything.

Please know that my entire family is so appreciative of all that you did and we all realize that you took a special interest in this case and you acted with your heart as well as your expertise.

I hope that I will never need your services again but if I do I will not hesitate to call you.

I love cases that end with very satisfied clients. I wrote a very complimentary letter to the sheriff concerning the actions of his deputy who took down a meth lab. The sheriff assured me he would put it in the deputy's personnel file and commend him for his actions.

The blurb on the back cover of this book by this client reads, *"If this book had been available for my daughter she might have been able to avoid homelessness, drug addiction, physical and emotional abuse from a man she thought she knew."*

ALCOHOL

We haven't really talked about addiction to alcohol. As most people know, alcohol can be just as addictive as prescription drugs, cocaine, heroin, and crack. But how do you know if your new friend "has a drinking problem" or if he is just a good-time guy? It might be difficult to tell. I've spoken with psychologists, experts in dealing with patients' alcohol problems.

Five signs to watch for. If you are on only your second or third date these signs may not be readably apparent.

1. We spoke before about a person's driving record. Two DUIs, in my opinion, is a sign that the person has a problem. If you can get someone to run his driving history and you find he has more than one DUI, watch out.

2. If your new date can drink you under the table, that is, if he consumes a large amount of alcohol but never really seems drunk, watch out. A high tolerance to alcoholic beverages is a sign that he might be addicted.

3. If he tells you he's going to stop drinking—probably to prove to you that he doesn't have a problem—and gets withdrawal symptoms like nausea, sweating, shakiness, and anxiety, then he's got a problem.

4. If he starts drinking in the morning (and hides that from you) and drinks a little all day, then there's an issue.

5. If you've been with him longer than just a few dates and you've already complained about his drinking too much; and you find that he's hidden alcohol around the house, perhaps a bottle of vodka under the bathroom sink or maybe not even the whole bottle because he's afraid you'll notice it missing; or he's poured some in a glass and hides that glass somewhere that he can get to and you're unlikely to find, he's got a problem.

Are there other signs of alcohol addiction? Sure, but rather then go into all of the possibilities here, I'd suggest a trip to a counselor or that take your new friend to an AA meeting.

Addiction to alcohol is just as bad as an addiction to prescription drugs. The only real difference is that alcohol is easier to obtain. He can walk into any liquor store or bar and get what he "needs" without fear of being arrested.

THE SHORT LIST

♦ When your new date pulls out the **cocaine** and puts a line down for you to snort, that's a big red flag.

♦ If he offers you **a pill** to relax, don't take it. He may even pop one in his own mouth to prove to you that there's nothing there that is going to harm you.

♦ If you're **embarrassed** to introduce him to your friends or family, consider why. Is it his drug use or drinking?

♦ If he exhibits **any of the five signs** above **of alcohol addiction**, beware.

CHAPTER 8

THE FINAL EXAM

A private investigator from Israel called me at 7:00 A.M this morning and woke me up. He has a female client that wants to know if a certain male Israeli who lives in south Florida is married or not. Can I find out for his client?

What does that sound like to you? Could be a Nigerian Scam if he's asking for money for plane tickets back to Israel. Or it could be she met the guy while she was traveling in the U.S. and now has more than a casual interest in him and while he claimed he was single, she's not so sure. Any of that sound familiar?

Hopefully before this book goes to press we'll have the answer. The point, of course, is that as soon as you read the above paragraph, hopefully you were already looking suspiciously at this person and asking yourself the same questions I asked.

TEST SITUATION ONE

Matt, a single guy in his early twenties began dating Valerie who was a stripper/pole dancer at a local strip joint. She quickly became pregnant and they had a child. After having the child she went back to stripping. The tips were too good to pass up.

A year later they had a heated argument and Valerie called the police saying that Matt had hit her and she was afraid. The police showed up and arrested Matt on a domestic violence charge.

There are a couple of Murphy Laws on sex that cover this situation.

1. *Never sleep with anyone crazier than yourself.*

2. *Never lie down with a woman who has more troubles than you.*

Previous to this argument Valerie told Matt that her friend had made up a domestic violence charge against her husband and had him arrested on it. When they had arguments, Valerie would threaten Matt with calling the police. Finally one night, according to Matt, she went through on her threat.

Matt was carted off to jail and charged with domestic violence. He claimed he never struck Valerie and she was lying.

Okay, now for the test. Who should have done a little premarital background on whom before their relationship became too involved?

The answer of course is they both should have. Had they done that, Matt would have seen that Valerie had a long string of traffic charges against her which resulted in her losing her driver's license twice. Also, when you think about stripping as an occupation, it really is one big lie, isn't it? In the process of taking ones clothes off for money, the stripper is sort-of promising the onlookers that maybe more could be had under the right circumstances. Am I suggesting that all strippers are hookers, no. But the stripping is, in its own way, a bit dishonest. Hanging the bait out but not letting the fish bite.

After Matt's arrest and release from jail pending trial, Valerie repeatedly attempted to contact Matt, telling his parents that if he would just call her she would "drop the charges." Makes you wonder if in fact the charges were really bogus as Matt claimed? Matt didn't have any previous arrests.

Valerie is now living with a new boyfriend. I did some background on the boyfriend because we're now looking at a child custody case. Guess what? The new boyfriend had a domestic violence arrest a year ago in another state. This sort of follows the typical pattern of abused women—going from one abusive relationship to another.

Matt still maintains his innocence even though Valerie appeared in court with an undated photograph of her with a black eye. Did Matt give it to her? I really don't know. He denies it. Did the new boyfriend give it to her? That's anyone's guess.

I obtained a list of the addresses where Matt and Valerie lived together and pulled the log of 911 calls and police responses to those addresses during the appropriate time frame when they were there together. There were several calls and police responses to those addresses for various reasons. When I see that, it makes me understand exactly how stormy their relationship was.

When I preformed the background check on Valerie I really didn't find anything other than the string of traffic tickets, which might not have disqualified her. But they are both young, early twenties, so give them ten years and let's see how things change. You'll find that those that are very young often won't have records. But sometimes they do, and it's worth the effort to search.

TEST SITUATION TWO

Allie was a very pretty girl. She had her CPA and but she'd long had the desire to attend law school. She went to work for as an in-house bookkeeper/accountant for a small firm with about twenty employees. Previously she had worked for one of the big eight accounting firms. The employer, Benjamin, checked her personal and professional references and they all said nice things about Allie. What Ben didn't do was any sort of criminal or driving history on her.

Early on several of Ben's employees came to him and said they thought Allie was doing some drugs on the job. Ben confronted Allie about it and she admitted that she had prescriptions from her doctor for Xanax and heartburn medication. Ben was fairly naïve and thought that since she had the prescription for Xanax from a doctor, what could he do as long as it didn't interfere with her job performance?

What did interfere with her job performance was the attraction between the two of them. Ben was married but Allie was single, very sexual, and ten years younger than Ben. It wasn't very long before Ben and Allie began an affair. What Ben didn't know was that Allie was also an alcoholic. In hindsight, Ben realized that the references that Allie put on her resume were probably men that she had slept with. That sort of thing won't show up on a background check.

What would have shown up had Ben bothered to check, were a string of driving infractions including DUIs which led to two other infractions of driving while her license was suspended. She also had two civil complaints by creditors and one misdemeanor charge for a worthless check, which was later dismissed.

As it turned out, Ben, who was basically a non-drinker, was now heavily involved with Allie, the alcoholic. He even gave Allie a company car to drive, which she promptly wrecked twice within ten days while she was drunk.

One evening early on in their relationship, Allie was drunk as usual and called Ben's wife and told her that she was sleeping with Ben. This quickly prompted a very expensive divorce for Ben and his wife. His wife took the three kids and moved out of state.

Ben continued to date, sleepover with, but not live with Allie for two more years. Finally he wised up and during one of her rants as they were driving near the beach, Allie insisted on getting out of the car. She'd tried to throw herself out of the car while they were driving down the freeway on more than one occasion. Ben pulled to a stop in a parking lot, Allie slammed the door behind her and yelled that she never wanted to see him again. She threw her purse at the back of the car as he drove away.

Subsequently, Allie called him periodically but he refused to see her. Allie began going to AA meetings, she had gone previously but had always "slipped." In fact Ben put her in rehab after two previous binges, but she began drinking again as soon as she was out. After their breakup, Allie quit drinking. She went to law school and received her law degree and now works as an attorney.

Ben gave serious consideration to marrying Allie, and she wanted a child. His fear was that she wouldn't maintain her sobriety and he'd come home from work one day and she would be passed out on the couch and the child would be running wild, unattended. Allie later became pregnant by someone she met at an AA meeting. They married but divorced after less than a year. While she was staying sober, the new husband could not, and Allie had the good sense to end it before she'd been married to him for too long. She subsequently married another attorney. She has been sober for a dozen years.

Go through Ben and Allie's story and look at all of the heartache and money that could have been saved had Ben only done a more thorough background check on Allie. Personal references are not enough. They may be a good start for finding out about a person's character, but you need to dig more. After that you can evaluate all of the facts you've gathered and make your decision. Stay alert to the five things women need to know about the men they date. Some of these will only show after the relationship develops a little deeper. If they appear, don't hesitate to walk away from the relationship.

THE SHORT LIST

◆ Is the **divorce** final or is he still **married**?

◆ Does he have **his own money** or is he living in his mother's basement?

◆ Have you **searched criminal records** in the counties where he has lived for the past ten years?

◆ Does he use illegal substances, **cocaine, marijuana to excess, meth, prescription drugs?**

◆ Is he an **abuser of alcohol?** Can he drink you under the table? Watch for the signs.

Made in the USA
San Bernardino, CA
09 March 2017